A Lady CALLED MOM

M.A. BENJAMIN

AuthorHouse™
1663 Liberty Drive
Bloomington, IN 47403
www.authorhouse.com
Phone: 1 (833) 262-8899

Because of the dynamic nature of the Internet, any web addresses or links contained in
this book may have changed since publication and may no longer be valid. The views
expressed in this work are solely those of the author and do not necessarily reflect the views
of the publisher, and the publisher hereby disclaims any responsibility for them.

This book is printed on acid-free paper.

ISBN: 978-1-7283-6964-8 (sc)
ISBN: 978-1-7283-6965-5 (e)

Library of Congress Control Number: 2020914629

Print information available on the last page.

Published by AuthorHouse   09/04/2020

authorHOUSE®

Contents

Have you ever wondered…

What exactly does being a mom entail?

Dedicated to our mom
Marian M McD
1938-2018

We may not have always said it
but we did our best to show you
that we were eternally grateful
to have been blessed with you
as our mom.

A Daughter, Sister, Niece, Aunt, Wife,
an In-Law, Cook, Evangelist, Mother,
Constant giver, Seamstress, Teacher,
Grandmother, Great Grandma

You wore many hats in your lifetime.
At time we thought you mean
At many more times with love
but no matter which part of the spectrum
you were on, YOU were loved
and definitely are missed.

Being A Mom

This is the hardest job in the world.
You literally have to become everything
You have to do everything
Most importantly, you had to try to keep from killing us as we grew.

That tiny being you have just given birth to
That tiny trusting child will grow up
Along the way they will try your patience to the bitter end
After all we have a little bit of you within us…

You are our mother.
Each pregnancy
Each and every different craving
Each labor pain
Each child is completely different
So of course you would feel more for some than others
We failed to come equipped with that most important item
our very own individual instruction manual
You were our whole world
We hung on your every word.

You loved us unconditionally
You run when we would call or yell
You doctor us when we get hurt
You helped us study for exams
You helped with our homework
You were our everything until….
Puberty.

We started to realize you were not as ALL KNOWING as we thought
We started to realize there were other things happening
Other people we 'liked' but you said 'no'
Even though your patience was tried
Thank GOD we are still alive

You taught us well
We now walk the road you did
As you enjoy being a grandparent
Smiling all the time
It is now us ready to kill

You taught us by example
That is what we are attempting to do

Thank, you for being our mother, our teacher, our mom….

A Noble Woman

Proverbs 31 speaks of a noble woman
How she is praised by her family

As a wife
Yes, there were problems
Every single relationship has them
Not everyday is sunshine and roses
He regretted some of the things that happened
That's life
You did your best
You and dad lasted 42 years
You cared for him til the end

I know this because I'd spoken with dad about you
He had regrets about some things but he loved you
In his own words
>   *'If i had to do it all over again I'd still choose her,*
>   *He would treat you a lot better than he did'*
>   *He literally sang your praises*
>   *He made a great choice.*

As a mom
You gave birth and raised 8 of us
You and dad were outnumbered
Yet there were no babysitters, no nanny
You taught us what we need to know to better ourselves
When we were young your best friend was always handing off your neck
You kept us in line with it
You kept us learning about GOD as well
You had your own sense it humor

You were a daughter, sister, niece, cousin
You were a wife, soulmate
You were a mother, teacher, counselor
You were an even more serious child of GOD
You were a Proverbs 31 woman

Fashion Designer

What is fashion
How does it start
Usually as an idea
Many times it's simply a need

An idea begins to take form
Oh, the various items
Shirt, suit, pants, skirt, dress
The ideas never ends

What pattern should be used
Should it be A-Line, form fitting, or loose
Should I take the top of this one and the bottom of this
Wait, I think I can come up with my own pattern
Wow that garment would look fantastic
What fabric or fabrics would be required
What color should it be
Should it be plain, floral, stripes, polka dots
The options are limitless
How many yards would it require
Should you put a design on it
How thick of a thread should you use to embroider it
You would be off to the avenue and back before we could get into any trouble

Your were off.
Out came the pins, scissors and yard stick
No kids allowed in the room
There were times you sewed clothes all night long
You know how it was
Eight kids and we absolutely loved letting you know things last minute

Your reward
"What!, you made that for me"
No i wasn't scrunching up my face
No I didn't raise my voice.

There were times your creations were one of a kind
Wonderful, Fabulous, absolutely Gorgeous
Other times we cringed
Right before picture day
You'd create a large hair piece to accessorize the garment
Thank GOD you got better as we aged

Truth be told you taught us all to sew
Some of us won't admit it
You would sew and we would hem by hand
That's how we started before we could touch your machine.

You were our fashion coordinator.
Our own personal shopper
Our Fashion Designer

$\mathcal{S}$iblings

Siblings love each other dearly
You grow up together
You know more about each other than anyone else
The good and the bad
You know ALL the secrets...

You grow up
Leave home
Time goes by soo fast

So many times in life
We think of the other person
We say a quick prayer for them
I'll call later
So easy right...

Many times there's no time to text
Much less to write a letter or send an email
So much has happened
So much to tell
I'll call them later.

Life steps in
Things get pushed to the back burner
A day, a week, a month has passed
Where has the time gone
It's already their birthday
I'll wait and see them on the next holiday.

Time leads to separation
You haven't forgotten them
Love continues to endure
Memories help us to hold on

Wow I haven't seen you in how many years
Our hearts are warmed
The time just melts away
How easy put that other hat back on

Siblings just have that oh so special bond….

Mom

What can I say?
    Thank you?
        It just doesn't seem enough.
Thank you for my birth
    We know it was hard.
Thank you for my child hood
    We know it wasn't easy.
Thank you for my first apartment
    We know it came in handy.
Thank you, for being there as an adult.
    For you are
        Always there.
As I said:
    "Thank you, just doesn't seem enough.

I know I wasn't the easiest child to raise,
    Although I did think I was the most obedient (smile).
    After all you did have eight of us.
    But you set me straight on that one,
    I was complaining about my granddaughter
        You know—
            The one that looks like me.
    And you simply said—
        "Enjoy raising yourself", and then,
            you just started laughing at me.
That gave me a lot to think about
    But I still think I wasn't that bad
        you might have me mixed up
            with one of the others (smile)."

"You raised eight kids
  I know it wasn't easy—
    Hey, I was there for most of it.
We all had our own faults,
    our own idiosyncrasies.
Our different behaviors alone,
    would make any therapist happy.
You know how much money
    they would have made with us?
Good thing Dad worked for the city.

I know you were HAPPY,
  when school was in session
    A little break—
      a few hours of semi quiet.
But of course the drawbacks of that
    There was always someone still left at home.
    You had to get everyone up and out
      with a hot breakfast.
        On time
          Every Day!
        No school breakfasts served back then.
    Everyone needing help with homework
      The others still wanting their time
        At the same time.
    Getting us fed and back in bed on time.
    Our constant can we go here or there.
      That one was always easy though,
        The answer was usually "NO".
      If it wasn't educational,
        It usually wasn't going to happen.

And of course Your favorite:
        The germs WE brought home for you.

Oh yes, we were very generous in bringing home things to you:
        Chicken pox, measles, German measles,
        mumps, scarlet fever, wing worm;
        not to undermine all the colds,
        runny noses, and flu we spread.
Anything they were giving out at school,
    we brought home.
    Your all time favorite—
        the head lice.`
    All those heads to check and
        shampoo every two days.
    The pairs of stockings you would go through,
        You had to cut up just to cover our
        heads with once you've gone through
        them.
And of course—
    We spread them generously (smile)
    Isn't that what you taught us
        To share
            with our sisters and brothers.

The best part—
    was the bathroom.
        Remember at one time we only had one—
            one bathroom
        Two adults and six kids
            all sick trying to get in;
                and when we couldn't
                    well the floor worked as well.
Remember the Thanksgiving holiday,
    the whole house was sick?

It was just non-stop!
> *By the time you got the last one better*
> > *It went around again and again*
Well I did say you taught us to be generous.

Now lets not forget all that educational TV:
> *It was PBS, Disney, Animal Kingdom*
> > *or the news*
> > > *ALL DAY long!*
> *On occasion you did allow us to watch Chiller Theater*
> > *Cinderella, The Wizard of Oz etc*
> > > *NOTHING ELSE.*
"But then there was no cable back then
> *Our channels consisted of*
> > *Channels 2,4,7,11 & 13.*

And you did all this:
> *Twenty-four hours a day*
> > *Seven days a week*
> > *THREE HUNDRED SIXTY-FIVE OR*
> *SIXTY-SIX*
> > *Days a year!!*
> *You were better than the US Postal Service.*
> > *Sun, rain, sleet, snow, hail, blizzard*
> > > *No matter the weather outside,*
> > > > *YOU were always there.*
> > *School, doctors appointments,*
> > > *everything*
> *You had:*
> > *No nanny, NO daycare, No assistant.*
> *Dad worked outside and you worked inside.*
> *Back then it wasn't called "work",*
> > *But we know the truth."*

"But you did it,
  And amazingly
    You still have your sanity!
    Some of us are still trying to figure that one out.
    You still have your looks,
      No plastic surgery.
      Most people are surprised to know your age
    It's Grandma's genes—
      Our little secret.

I know I complained a lot about being the maid.
  Mostly to myself and the others
    I wasn't stupid, (smile).
Having to always help
  "Because I was the oldest"
But it gave me the skills I use today.
You always said—
  "When someone's taking the time to teach you
  something sit down and learn it.
    You never know when you'll need it"
  I apologize for anything I've ever done to you,
    And I'm quite sure,
      there are a few things I don't remember.
  But, all I can say is,
  Thanks MOM.

HATS OFF TO YOU, MOM
You are one hell of a LADY!
Enjoy your life
  You have deserved every vacation
    You can take
  You have deserved every day you can just sit down"

"You have deserved every day you can just sit down
   To just do nothing,
    To mess with your plants,
     Or just,
    To just make a cup of tea and read.
Just don't rest too much
  we still want you around
   for many more years. (smile)

I love you MOM."

The Disciplinarian

It was your way, or the highway.
No this is this
No this is why
What did I say!
End of statement..

We couldn't play both parents against each other
Dad let you have that rein,
You were the one at home with us
You knew us better than he did
He would rarely go against what you said

To us
You were simply MEAN
You didn't understand the way of things
To us you were old
How could you understand what's happening today
You grew up in ancient times.
Or so we thought...

Payback came in the form of your grandchildren
As you told me one day
'So, how do you enjoy raising yourself'
It took a while to understand
But hey, she had to be wrong
I would have never done these things to her
After all how could I have gotten away with it
she was always home..

Now that we are grown
Kids of our own
We became the MEAN ones
We fully understand everything you tried to do
The not letting us go places'
Some people are crazy out there
We didn't know
We just wanted to go with our friends
To us you simply didn't understand

Thank you for all the understanding you actually had
Thank you for keeping us safe to grow up and find out for ourselves.

Hats

I don't know where to start
You truly loved them
You had so many
You wore them each proudly
Every outfit had a matching hat, purse or clutch
Some even had specific shoes and gloves to go with them
No need to wait for Easter
For you those items were always a must.

You wore other hats as well
Many taken for granted by some
You were
    A Daughter, A Niece, A Sister, An Aunt,
    A Mother, A Wife, An In-Law, A Cook,
    An Accountant, A Decorator, A Shopper,
    A Teacher, A Seamstress, A Disciplinarian,
    A Giver, An Evangelist, A Singer
    A Grandmother (Ma as you preferred)
    A Great Grandmother
Many times your hat my get a little dusty
No problem
You'd just clean it off
Onward you would go like no time has passed

Yes My Lady,
You were many things at many times
But you always did your best to do it with grace and love.

Our Chef

I figured you are where I've gotten it from.
Making something out of nothing
We would say 'where did you get that!
*   I didn't see that in the kitchen'*
Your response, 'You have to know what you're looking at.'

How could a family with eight kids
Where the mother actually stayed home
Actually feed those growing kids properly
I have to admit we never missed a meal..
They didn't know you and dad
You guys bought meat by the quarter, half, or whole..

You were experimental to a fault
Always trying to find a new recipe for us
Always trying to figure out a new meal for us to try.
Almost everything was game
You'd figure out what it should taste like
Did we like it
If yes, off you went
It became a new food for us
Various versions would ensue
Until a favorite two or more could be found.
If it didn't work out
You always had the items for a quick meal set aside
Dinner was always at six.
You were amazing to watch in the kitchen
At least until it became our turn to cook

We know various ways to cook meats
The only day we didn't eat meat was Friday
That was fresh fish day
On occasion you would treat us to take out
You'd say
'You don't, really know what's in that food unless you make it yourself.'

Even raw vegetables
You found ways to make us eat salads
    long before they were considered fashionable
You know, even before they came prepackaged
When you had to cut each vegetable yourself to make it
You introduced various options before known
Bacon strips, chopped sausage, stewed chicken, shrimps
And of course cheeses, regular or melted

Cooking good food was your secret love affair
Actually it's a gift you've passed down to us all
And we have passed your love of food to the next generation
They simply think it's our love
But truth be told
    it's that part of you we continue to nurture
It's another part of you we continue pass to the next generation
Yes, You still live in ALL of us!!!

Mother

MOM
Your hours of labor thought to be unappreciated
Are greatly appreciated
Without you I wouldn't exist
Wouldn't be able to thank you
To give you grands and future great grands
To care for you and love you

OUTSTANDING PERSON
No matter what life throws you -
You are always ready
You always overcome
You have taught us to love others
How to handle various situations in life

TEACHER
From birth to present
You are still trying to teach us
Even as we try to care for you
That teacher in you is still going
Even when life thought it had you down
But you showing even life that there is so much more to you
You simply bounced back
Not completely yet
But I know you are on your way

HEALER
Never a person for regular medicines
Unless it tasted horrible
Then it was A-OK for us to take
You favored the herbs and minerals verses chemical medicines
To give you credit
> *We were never sick for long*
You definitely have the touch

EVERLASTING AND ETERNAL
The love you gave us as kids has grown leaps and bounds
I know we don't always call, visit or write
To be honest you don't check email
So actually we Have to call or visit
We love you immensely
You still see and try to correct our errors
We laugh
Even though we tower above you
You still see the child within us
No matter how old we get
You will be eternally in our hearts

Realist
You never mince words
You knew the friends we should and shouldn't keep
You made us study
    Even when we had no homework
Most importantly
You taught us and our kids about GOD
We may not always do as we should
But believe me
HE DOES LIVE WITHIN US

What can I say?
You are one in a million
You are our MOTHER

$\mathscr{S}$top Fading

You birth how many children
Helped us care for how many grandchildren
Proud MA of how many great grands
No one had ever call you grandma
No way not you
You were too young looking
Too full of energy
Sooo full of life

Your love of shopping and travel
So much embedded in all of us
Girls and boys alike

Those were the fun days

Caring for you is so hard to do
But not for the reason you think
On a daily basis I see you fading farther away
At times you come back with your fight
Your fight to stay alive

Sometimes we argue
mostly because at times I think you are trying to give up
That is absolutely not allowed
I don't care how much we argue
At least it tells me you still have fight in you
It gives me hope

The doctor visits hurt because it's reality kicking the door in
A reminder that we are all human
That we are all on a clock
One day that clock will stop working

I just want to keep you around for as long as possible

Keep fighting
Keep giving those doctors and nurses hell
Just hurry back home
Stop scaring me
Stop fading away

National Sibling Day

McDaniel
"8"

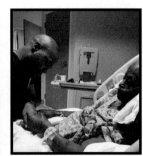

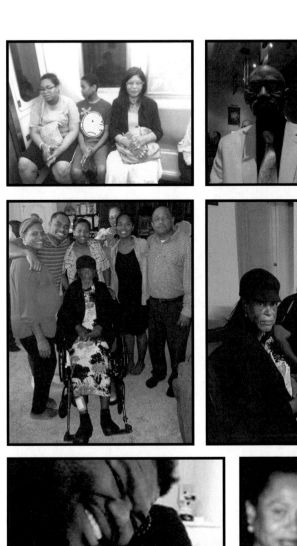

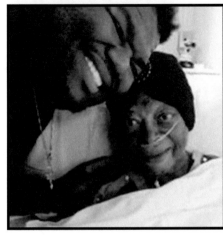

Health

As a youth you get sick
A trip to the doctor is scary
Yes, we all hated the shots
They made you tired
You got angry
You slept

You have lived your life
You have raised your kids
It's now time to retire
Time to rest
To do what you want
Time to live your life.

What's going on here?
Oh my,
The aches and pains that appeared
What's happening now
I can't read that..

The scariest one..
The chest pain
So many possibilities
Problem you only have one heart
Is it just gas or something else
If you're lucky you have a great doctor
One who knows what they're doing

We take our health for granted
We pray that pain will go away
I'll just take a nap.
Who needs physicals
Just a waste of time and money
So we think

The problem is as we age we find we go more often
This is my time
I don't want to waste it in a waiting room

No matter our age
Our health should always come first
If you don't care for you
You can't possibly properly care for others…

Perfection

Something you taught us to strive for
Something you taught us to want to achieve
You try anyway
As long as you can breathe
You can continue to try
You can continue to achieve.

Your secrets to perfection
Knowing you can't achieve it without GOD
It usually requires someone's help along the journey
    Don't be afraid to ask
Never forget who helped and how you got there
DO NOT step on others
    GOD will take you there.

GODS definition
Treat others as you would like to be treated
Love one another as Christ loves the church.

We didn't have many friends
There was eight of us
Didn't need that many

The secret NO ONE ever achieves complete perfection
Help one another
NEVER stop achieving.

Oh, The Possibilities

As with any young child so full of promise
So Inquisitive
Always wanting to know the
*   'who, what, where, when, why and how'*
At least what's what we were told'
Grandma didn't say much if it didn't have to do with GOD
You did good in school and sang in church
We know that for sure
We've heard the story of the beautiful singing Benjamin Sisters

If it were another date and time
Your possibilities would have been endless.
You didn't let very much stop you.
When you were stopped it wasn't from lack of trying

You taught us all
Boys and girls alike
We literally almost learned everything you knew
You constantly talked the 'what ifs'
You weren't allowed to give up if you didn't try.

Then one day you got up
With a neighbors help
You signed yourself up for school
you went and got yourself a nursing license
Next thing we knew you were working
You were unstoppable.

As we grew
You grew
You taught us
There is NO LIMIT to the possibilities of life
As long as we have GOD in front of us leading the way

To your grandkids, great grandkids and future generations of you'
We your eight pass the torch on to them

Oh the possibilities of those future generations
As long as they stay with Father GOD

Big Ma

You had your rules
Call me what?!
Grandma. No way
It's Ma or Big Ma

You refused to show
Or to let people know your true age
If you could have kept it from us you would have.

Your wardrobe Always ready to go

Wrinkles
I don't recall them appearing until your late 50s
But then as your kids
We weren't really looking
You were just mom
We were too consumed with our own lives
Yet secretly hoping we'd inherited those 'good' genes
You know
The ones that make you smile when people underestimate your age

Posture
Straight as an arrow
What!
You'd better be sitting up straight
If you didn't want to hear about back problems when you are older
I've taught you better!

Excersize
We marveled
You were 72 years of age
Always on the go
Walking 2-3 miles 2-3 days a week
We'd call you're getting back from a walk downtown and back
You tried daily to keep it up
Leg and arm Exercise
Squats, sit ups,
What-your skins not the same
All we could say was
'Where does she get that energy"
We were tired just listening to you

Youth
Teach them everything you know
Let them learn from our mistakes
We look at your photos
You teaching not only us but our children and grandchildren
Reading, math and of course stories from the Bible

We pray one day Father GOD will allow us to live to see even more generations
To impact them as you've done for us and ours

You truly were BIG MA

That Perfect Parent

Oh, her kids are so lucky
She seems to do everything right
How does she do it?

What!
I didn't know that!
How could children turn out like that?
You know how it is..
No discipline..
That child just needs a good _____!

So simple..
Or is it...
Everyone had an idea
Everyone had his/her opinions

Their eyes staring at you..
The hushed conversations when they see you..
The theories that are spoken of..
Yes,
The books that have been written...

Every parent started out as a kid
You learned from your parents
You pick and choose which parts you want to carry forward

You didn't even think about it before
Not until YOUR child was on the way
I'm not going to do this

I'm not going to do that
Oh no, the child has arrived
I think I'm ready
Everything is going great until
The child has made friends
The child is influenced by them
Will they or won't they still obey you....

Parenthood is a guaranteed 100% shot in the dark
The child DID NOT come with instructions
You learn about them
As they learn about you...

As a parent all you can do is
Install good moral values
Love and respect of themselves as well as others
Educate them.
It's truly not all left to the teachers
Don't forget the most important
It's ok to say NO
The more you give the more they will want
They need to learn the value of some things
Most kids once grown don't think of the money
They remember the good and bad times
Time spent is the most valuable..

The secret to the perfect parent...
There is NO PERFECT PARENT.

Do your best
Seek GOD for help with everything.

Once they are grown
You'd be amazed at the person standing before you....

That Mighty Warrior

The lessons you taught
The patience you had
The hope you instilled

The lessons unlearned
The times patience was lost
At times hope seemed futile

You prayed
You regrouped
You started again

Your love never ended
Your prayers never stopped
When things were crazy
When times were hard
You simply prayed all the more

Praying harder and harder never relenting
When we wouldn't listen
When we refused to obey
When we KNEW better
You prayed
You prayed all the time
You prayed with every breath
You prayed even to your last breath

YOU showed us what a mighty warrior is
YOU showed us how a mighty warrior lives
YOU showed us the truth

Moms are more than just mom
Moms are GODS Mighty Prayer Warriors

We love and miss you terribly…

*J*ust Thinking....

I'm just sitting here looking around
Missing you soo much
Longing to talk to you
To hear your laugh
Or even one of your arguments
Believe that..
I actually miss that

On occasion I still jump up
Yes, Ma I'm coming
Or on a sleepy morning I've caught myself
'Why can't she sleep late?'

Then I feel horrible
It was just my imagination
Although at times it's so so real

You aren't here for me to cook breakfast or any other meal for
You are asleep
Only a sleep you will never wake up from
Not on this side anyway

I know you are no longer on pain
I know you are happy talking with family long past
But…..

Anyway,
I just wanted you to know
I'm just thinking about you….

Love and miss you sooo much.

Mommy

Your passing has left such a whole in my heart
I can't truly explain it

We didn't always agree on things
But then who does
You had eight of us
You raised us mostly by yourself since dad was always working
You taught us to be self sufficient,
Reliant on no one but GOD and family

Even in our grown years you were always there
Attempting to guide us
Still trying to care for us
Still trying to steer us from unknown dangers
Even when you were the one needing the care
You never gave up on us
Even with your crooked finger moving in the air
Holding the other hand to your chest
As you were trying to make a point to us
To do something a certain way
What can I say
You still saw the child in us

As we wondered where that strong woman was disappearing to
Right before our eyes
You'd get mad at us when we'd tell you
"That's it, keep that fight in you going"
You'd even have to laugh at it sometimes yourself
For us it meant you hadn't given up yet
You'd still fight for the right to live
No matter what the doctors said
"She's lived a good life"
You often told us once you reach a certain age doctors and hospitals give up on you
After all you knew.
You'd worked in a hospital for years
Mom you were and still are loved by so many
Missed so much on a daily basis
We love you

rayer

As mommy would say

Simply get on your knees and talk to Jesus as if he was standing right in front of you. He already knows your faults so there is no need to lie or try to hide it.. just be truthful. The best part - No matter what you could have done. Even murder. HE WILL NOT TURN YOU AWAY.

LORD JESUS you died on the cross for my *(your name),*sins. I ask for your forgiveness. I ask that you come into my heart and become my Lord and Savior. FATHER GOD thank you for becoming the GOD of my life. In Jesus name I pray. Amen.

Welcome guys. Ma and the rest of the family that has already transitioned over is waiting for us when we get there.

I hope you guys enjoyed the book.

References

HCSB. Holman Christian Standard Bible.

Mom. From the HEART

Mother. LIFE

Printed in the United States
By Bookmasters